I0096213

Sociocracy For All is a nonprofit operating globally and registered in
Massachusetts, USA. www.sociocracyforall.org
All content is licensed under a CC-SA-BY-NC license. 2023
ISBN: 978-1-949183-27-6
Ted Rau (2023). Guide for serving in circle roles.
A booklet for leaders, delegates, secretaries and facilitators in sociocracy

Table of contents

Introduction

Welcome!

This booklet is intended for sociocratic organizations that want to offer extra support to new people in process roles. We assume that new people in sociocratic organizations will get basic training to be well-oriented and empowered. However, process roles can benefit from a few extra reminders! For example, a new member might have received training as they entered the organization, but they get selected into a process role (delegate, secretary, leader, facilitator) for the first time months later. Note that the words and terms used might differ between organizations, as well as their exact role description. For example, the process of preparing an agenda might differ between organizations and even between circles in the same organization. In that sense, this is a refresher and an overview to be specified as needed.

Ted

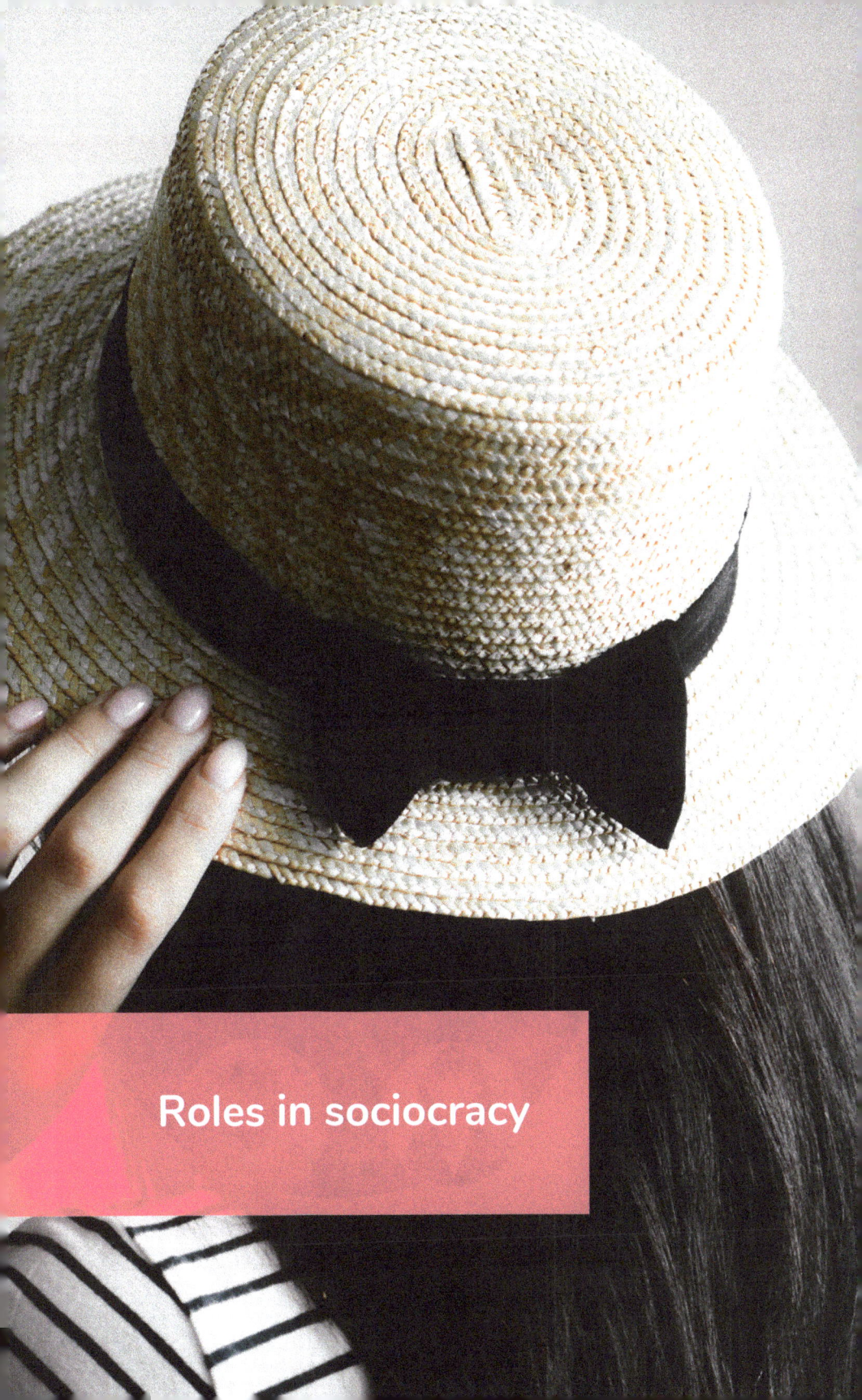

Roles in sociocracy

What are roles?

In a sociocratic organization, a circle is a semi-autonomous and self-organizing unit. Each circle typically has four key roles, each with specific responsibilities - leader, delegate, secretary, facilitator.

These roles work together to ensure that the circle functions smoothly and effectively. They help balance the power within the circle, prevent the concentration of power, and ensure efficient, inclusive decision-making.

Sociocracy For All

How roles work with the circle

The circle chooses who serves in the role, typically using the selection process where circle members nominate people and then decide by consent who is filling what role.

Every person fills the role for a certain time period, called the term. At the end of the term, a new decision is made, again by consent. In sociocracy, nothing prevents the circle from choosing the same person for the same role again; the circle's decision might depend on several considerations, like qualifications, performance, how many other people are qualified to do the role, and whether the circle thinks that a new constellation of circle roles supports the circle.

Circle roles act on behalf of the circle with the limits set by the circle in policy, role descriptions and workflows.

A leader, for example, might make decisions on behalf of the circle in the realm of circle operations, and a facilitator has a part in making and choosing proposals. People using sociocracy are comfortable with that level of power because they trust that people work towards the best of the circle, and that a distribution of power through roles supports empowerment and effectiveness.

It doesn't serve the circle if people in roles **don't** step into the power they have been given. A healthy way to fill a role is to work with the trust of the circle, self-responsibility, transparency and curiosity and openness to feedback on how the role is filled.

The difference between an autocratic rule and people filling a role is (1) that the person only fills the role for a certain term, (2) that they are selected by consent (3) that they are bound by circle and organizational policy (4) that there are feedback processes in place.

Sociocracy For All

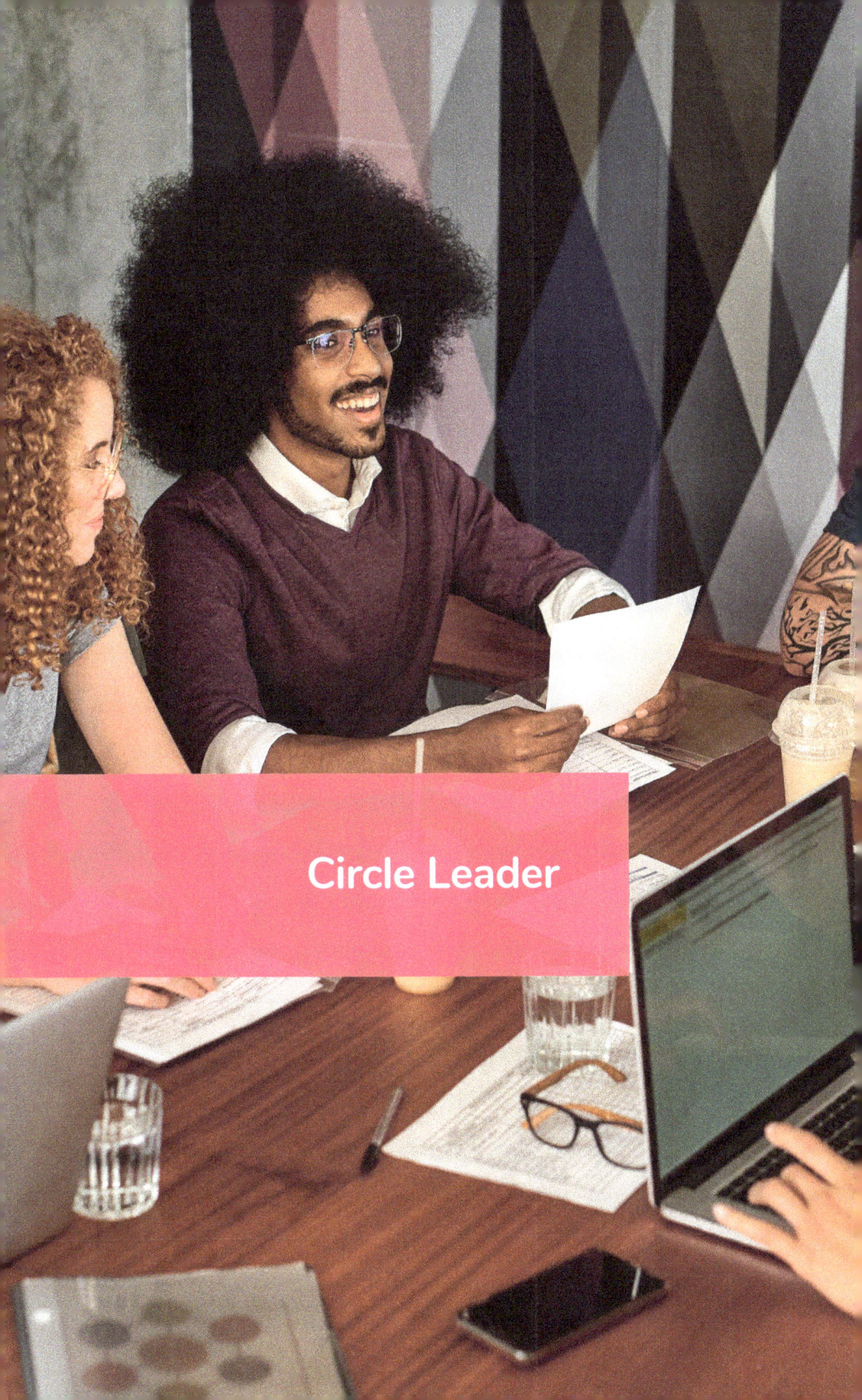
Circle Leader

The circle leader

(other names:
coordinator; steward,
coach, lead link, guide)

What does a leader do?

Leaders do two things at once:

- Leaders hold an operational role: supporting the circle's work
- Leaders hold a process-related role: connecting the wider organization to the circle.

Leadership in a circle is a responsibility with a lot of opportunity. Like the coach of a winning team!

Supporting operations

As a leader, it's your job to make sure everything in the circle gets done. That doesn't mean you're supposed to do everything.

Instead, your role is to pay attention to the productivity and flow of the tasks in your circle's domain.

Notice what doesn't get done.

Assigning tasks

Are all the pieces of the work clearly assigned? If not, the leader needs to pick up what is falling through the cracks and find a home for it.

- If the task fits into an existing role, then the leader passes it on to the role holder.
- If the task does **not** fit into an existing role, the leader might take care of it or make sure to create the clarity of who is performing the task. That might mean to initiate the forming of a role.

Time-critical decisions

A circle leader can make decisions between meetings that require immediate action. Generally, that is when an operational decision needs to be made because there is no existing policy or role that guides the decision at hand.

But it can also happen that a leader needs to approve exceptions to exiting policy due to unforeseen circumstances.

It is expected that the leader communicates proactively and transparently in those cases and with as much feedback from circle members as time allows.

Surfacing tensions

Observe and evaluate the practices and habits of the team. Is there something that's not working? Something that's in the way? Are there unquestioned assumptions or unhealthy patterns that need to be addressed?

Then make sure to put those topics on the agenda so the circle can find solutions.

Accountability

Just because a task is assigned doesn't always mean it gets done... unfortunately!

Someone might be running into unexpected challenges, avoid the task or simply forget. Check in with your team and support them so everyone can do what they signed up to do.

Sociocracy For All

Linking and reporting

Another role as the leader is to serve as link between the circle and its parent circle.

In the parent circle meetings, ask yourself:
How do the things that we talk about here affect my circle?

In your circle meetings, ask yourself: What does my circle need to know about what's going on in the rest of the organization?

This is important because information flow between parent circles and sub-circles keeps the alignment between the different parts of the organization. Thinking about who needs to know needs attention!

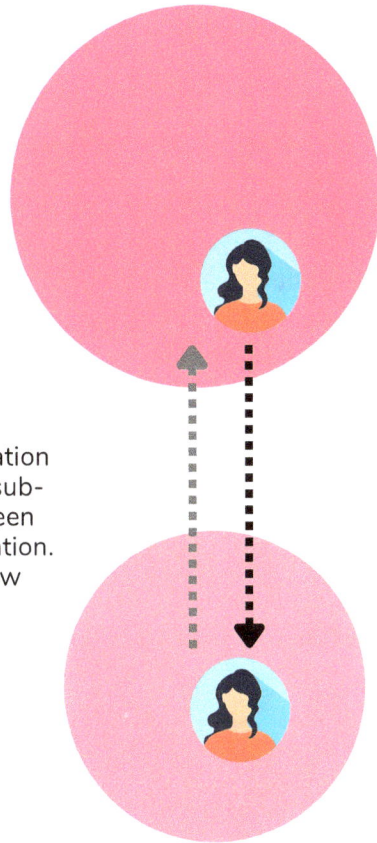

Useful mantras for leaders

Self-responsibility

- "It's my job to help others do the best they can."
- "If something isn't working, I will work to address it instead of complaining or blaming others. Maybe there's a proposal I could prepare? "
- "When others tell me about their experience, I might learn something that might help me get a better sense of the the whole."
- "Maybe I should check in to see if they need anything."

Responsibility of others

- "It's ok if others do things in their own way. What matters is the quality of the final result."
- "I don't have to do it alone - my support system is right around me!"

Common questions about leadership

How is the leader different than the facilitator?

The **leader** is in charge of the doing, and the facilitator is in charge of the talking **about** the doing. The leader is in charge of making sure operations happen (depending on the domain. For example: emails are written, fences are built, websites are functioning, articles are written, clients are contacted etc.).

The **facilitator** is in charge of structuring meetings and making sure everyone's input can be heard at a time when it's productive.

I still don't know what to actually DO now that I'm leader.

Sure! That makes sense. And in a perfect world, you didn't have to do anything because everyone would just know what to do and do it. In that perfect world, you would not be needed.

But sometimes things don't get done because people forget or have some emotional block or they don't have what they need to perform the task. Or it's simply not clear who needs to do it.

So: pay attention. Ask people what they need. See what is happening or not happening. Feel your way into where there might be lack of clarity that keeps progress from happening.

So, is there a hierarchy?

People often think of sociocracy as a system without bosses or hierarchies.

However, it **does** have a kind of hierarchy, but it's not about who's the boss. Instead, it's about the different jobs and responsibilities that exist in the organization, (which are grouped into different circles). Each circle focuses on a specific set of tasks and makes decisions related to those tasks. But, being in a higher or lower circle doesn't make one more important than the other; they just focus on different things. This helps everyone know who's doing what, which makes things work smoothly.

In sociocracy, nobody has power over anybody else. Instead, there's a system where every circle is connected to others, and decisions can only be made if everyone agrees. This stops any one person or group from having too much power and makes sure that everyone knows what's happening in different circles. Leaders in this system aren't like typical bosses. They're there to make sure everything gets done, but they have to follow the rules set by the circle, just like everyone else. Also, in sociocracy, roles are tied to the tasks of a circle, not to individuals. This means that one person can have many roles in different circles, depending on what they're good at and interested in.

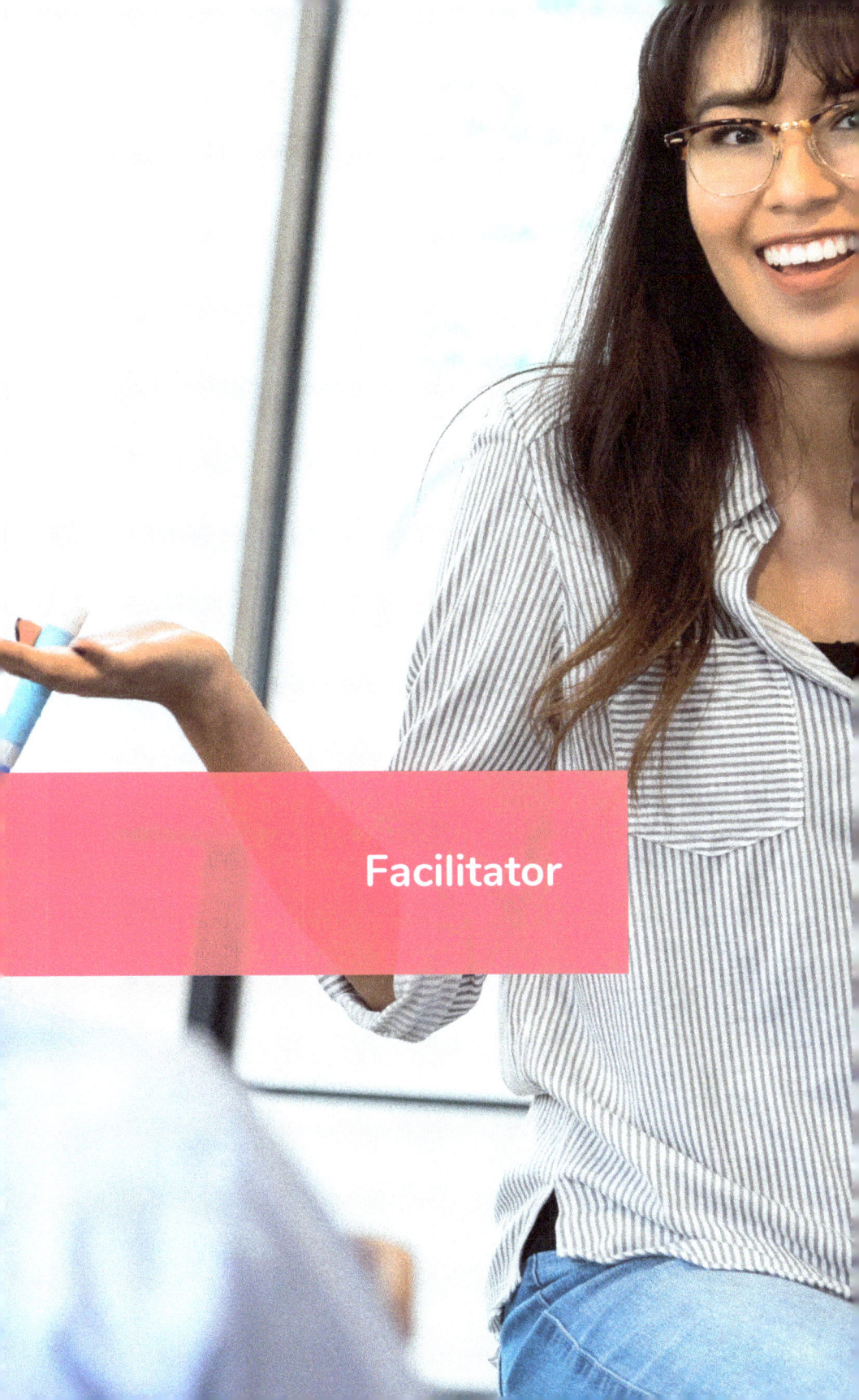

Facilitator

Facilitators

(other names: moderator, process guide)

What do facilitators do?

The role of the facilitator is pretty straightforward:
- prepare circle meetings
- moderate circle meetings

How the agenda for circle meetings gets prepared depends on your internal workflow - it might be very leader-driven, or agendas might be prepared by the secretary or the facilitator.

No matter who prepares agendas, it's universally true that a facilitator should understand the agenda they are facilitating.

A basic frame in sociocracy is to understand the difference between reports, explorations and decisions (on the right).

Reports

- An agenda item where information is shared.
- The facilitator makes sure everyone receives and understands the information by facilitating questions and answers.

Exploration

- An agenda item where a group gathers ideas and reactions in response to a problem or topic.
- The facilitator makes sure everyone's ideas are heard and, if needed, collected in writing.

Decision

- An agenda item where a decision clarifies the shared course of action.
- The facilitator makes sure a proposal is formed and approved, and that its implementation is on the way.

Supporting meetings

Facilitators balance efficiency and process.

- Sometimes what's needed is a pragmatic proposal so the groups can move on.
- Sometimes a situation calls for slowing down.

While it's impossible to know which is the right thing to do, it helps to be aware of both options and be intentional in our choices.

The basic tools that a facilitator should know are:

- rounds
- the meeting format of check-in/ADMIN, consenting to agenda, agenda, and meeting evaluation
- picture-forming and proposal shaping to write proposals together
- the consent process to make decisions
- strategies to integrate objections
- the selection process to select roles
- formats for review processes
- reflective listening

Sociocracy For All

Working with other roles

Working with the leader

- The leader should support the meeting, and the meeting should support the leader's task of moving the circle forward. That's why it's good to collaborate on planning agendas.
- The leader can be your go-to person in the meeting. If you think someone should make a proposal, consider asking the leader.

Working with the secretary

- Facilitators can support the secretary in writing down proposals, and the secretary will support the facilitator by typing proposals and confirming the wording.
- Using the backlog: A facilitator can ask the secretary to put new topics or questions into the backlog so everyone can stay focused on the current topic.

Useful mantras for facilitators

- "Let's aim for good enough, not perfect."
- "Let's do a round on this topic!"
- "Ok, does anyone have a proposal?"
- "I don't need to solve it. My job is only to help the group figure it out together."

Integrating objections:
- Amend: find a modification that avoids the objection.
- Concern: find a way to measure what you're concerned about so you have an early warning system.
- Term: shorten the term so you can evaluate what happens.

First aid for meetings

What if something goes sideways?
Here are a few ideas!

- **For yourself**
  - A moment of silence. (So you can think!)
  - Self-empathy and honest self-expression - share with your circle what you're struggling with.
- **For another person (that might be struggling)**
  - Reflect back what you heard them say and ask if you understood them correctly.
  - Ask how the circle can best support them.
- **For the circle**
  - Do a round on where people are at right now. (That also buys you time.)
  - Restate what has been said so far to check for understanding and clarity.
- **For the topic**
  - Form a small group to work on an issue until next meeting.
  - Delegate writing up a proposal.
  - Make a proposal and move to consent!

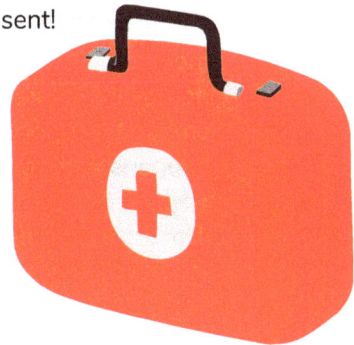

Common questions about leadership

?

Does the facilitator have to make all the proposals and answer all the questions?

No. The facilitator's job is just to make sure there is a proposal and that there are answers to clarifying questions. Making proposals on process will often come from facilitators and that helps the group.

Oftentimes, facilitators go into the "savior-trap", thinking that they have to manage everything. That gets exhausting! Facilitators will be more effective if they play questions or requests for proposals back into the group as often as possible.

?

Is the facilitator allowed to interrupt someone?

If the facilitator is acting in facilitator role (and not in member role), then yes. Interrupting others might be necessary to keep time, clarify, provide guidance and emotional support. This can be done more effectively if it happens with respect and transparency.

If a circle member who is facilitator interrupts someone to say something from member voice, it will likely be seen as overstepping the role which undermines trust.

In Sociocracy, how can one feel more comfortable with asserting authority as the facilitator?

Yes, the role of the facilitator comes with some authority and some responsibility. Yet, that doesn't mean a facilitator has to be authoritarian. There are two thoughts that might help facilitators who are uncomfortable with the authority they are given.

Your role is to create clarity on next steps. That doesn't mean that you decide but it's your job to make sure the circle has a chance to make progress. You are not in charge of making **all** the proposals but you have to make sure a proposal is made. For example, ask someone to make a proposal!

If there is a proposal on process, ask for consent. If you create an environment where it is safe to object, making a proposal is safe because people can say no and the proposal is not pushed onto the group. In our experience, most groups are very grateful when someone makes a concrete and useful proposal.

In Sociocracy, how much do facilitators participate or hold themselves back from a group making decisions?

Since facilitators are full members, they should not hold back at all, or their voice as circle members will not be heard.

What's important to alleviate the position of authority that some see facilitators in is to separate member voice and facilitator voice, e.g. by putting oneself in the middle of the round (instead of beginning or end of the round), or by clearly stating from what role they are speaking.

The Sociocracy For All website has meeting recordings and tons of resources for facilitators. Have a look.

There's also a booklet like this with an overview and checklists for the processes in sociocracy.

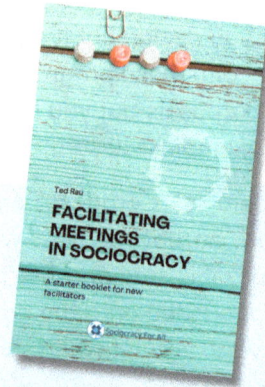

Get the book for facilitators!

sociocracyforall.org/books

Secretary

What do secretaries do?

The role of the secretary is a critical role in a circle, much more than note-taking!

(other names: admin, scribe, notetaker)

- Take notes during a meeting
- Make sure people have access to the notes
- Support the facilitator during the meeting
- Keeping the circle's documents orderly and accessible.

In a decentralized organization where decisions are made in many different places, note-taking is essential to ensure everyone knows what's happening. Notes need to be clear for people outside and inside of the circle.

- It's better to write less and summarize things well
- Offer to put new topics onto the backlog so the circle can avert distractions.

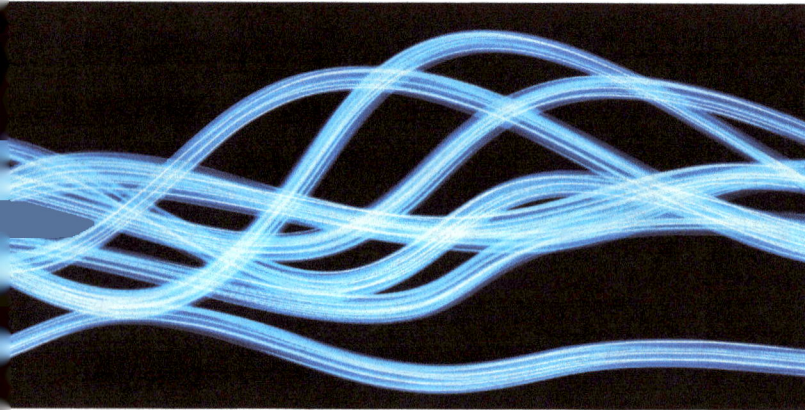

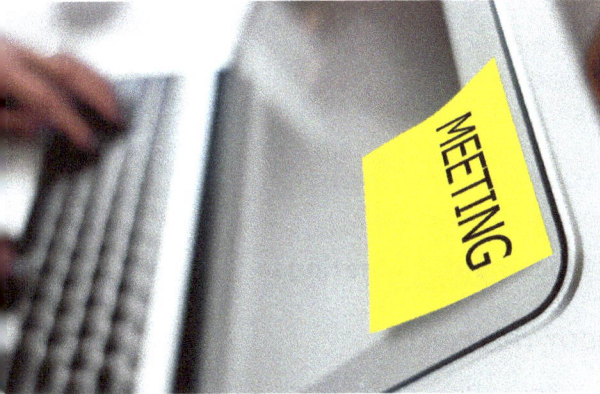

Supporting meetings

Good meeting notes include

- Attendance: who is present, who is not
- For reports: a quick summary of what was reported, plus relevant links.
- For explorations: all ideas summarized succinctly.
- For decisions:
  - the exact and final proposal
  - consent/objections (list objections)
  - the decision's term (when does the policy need to be reviewed)
- Next steps/who does what (unless they are recorded elsewhere)

It's typically unnecessary (and distracting) to record who said what.

Focus on ideas, not names.

An example of notes see page 28, 29, 30, 31.

Some secretaries wonder how much to type and how to organize an agenda document. Here's an example!

Coversheet (top of agenda document)

XYZ Circle Document & Meetings

ABOUT THIS CIRCLE

Aim(s)	Creating and selling XYZs	**Review Term**
Domain	XYZ IP and pricing; amazon KDE account	2022-11-22
Circle Members	Aaliyah (aaliyah@ABC.org); Carlos (carlos@ABC.org), Sakura (sakura@ABC.org), Nia (nia@ABC.org), Oliver (oliver@ABC.org)	
Parent Circle	Circle name & link to circle's document	
Sub-Circles	• Link	
Circle email address	XYZ@ABC.org	
Circle Folder	Link	
Objectives & Key Results	Sell 5000 copies in 2023	
Key Links		

ROLES

Process Roles	Name & email address	Review Term
Leader	aaliyah@ABC.org	2023-11-10
Delegate	nia@ABC.org	2024-04-18
Facilitator	carlos@ABC.org	2023-11-10
Secretary	oliver@ABC.org	2024-04-18

Operational Roles	Name & email address	Review Term
Amazon KDE management	sakura@ABC.org	2023-06-30
Sales oversight	carlos@ABC.org	2023-06-30
Customer service	oliver@ABC.org	2023-06-30
Design	aaliyah@ABC.org	2023-09-01
Packaging and supplies	nia@ABC.org	2023-09-01

See all the policy links and roles. It's within the secretary's role to keep those documents in order and organized so they can be found.

OTHER POLICIES

Policy Title	Brief Description	Term
Print Quality Assurance Policy		2023-12-31
Booklet Pricing and Discount Strategy		2024-07-31
Customer Service and Conflict Resolution Guidelines		2024-07-31

BACKLOG

Due date	Priority	Description	Desired Outcome	Holder
2023-06-30	!!! ▾	User Registration Enhancement	Exploration ▾	Carlos
	!! ▾	Shopping Cart Update	Report ▾	Aaliyah
	!! ▾	User Review and Rating System	Decision ▾	Nia
	~~!! ▾~~	~~Activate Booklet Preview Feature~~	~~Exploration ▾~~	~~Carlos~~
	! ▾	Search Functionality Improvement	Exploration ▾	Oliver
	! ▾	Combine roles of Customer service and packaging?	Exploration ▾	Aaliyah
2023-11-10	z▾	Role selections leader and facilitator	Report ▾	Aaliyah
2024-04-18	z▾	Role selections facilitator and delegate	Report ▾	Aaliyah

You can sort this table by due date by Format > Table > sort ascending

The backlog is the most important because it organizes the future attention of the circle. (One agenda item is crossed out because the circle talked about in the their current meeting.)

Meeting minutes

Now every meeting has a section **in the same** document.

2023-06-12			
TIME & DURATION	**MEETING'S LOCATION/LINK:**		**OUTCOME**
09:00	10	**OPENING ROUND / CHECK-IN** (no notes)	
09:10	5	**ADMIN**	
		Attendance – *who's here and filling roles?*	
		Facilitator: Carlos	**Secretary**: Oliver	**Leader**: Aaliyah	**Delegate**: ~~Nia~~ (sick)	**Other members**: Sakura	
		Duration – *does anyone need to leave earlier?* 60min	
		Minutes – *anything needing attention from the previous meeting's minutes?* nope	
		Information – *any announcements?* Organization-wide open strategy session July 1st!	
		Next meeting – *when and where?* 2023-06-26	
00:15	2	**CONSENT TO AGENDA**	Decision
00:17	3	**ACTION ITEMS ACCOUNTABILITY** – *noted from previous meeting*	Report
		☑ Tell website circle about bug with shopping carts (Aaliyah)	
		☐ Research European packaging options (Nia)	
00:20	10	**REPORTS**	Report
		Parent Circle Report – Leader: Aaliyah	
		• Reviewed budget	
		• Discussed Q3 strategy	
		Sub-Circles Report – Delegate: Carlos	
		• Did role selections and reviews	
		Op Roles & Projects Reports – Role/Project Holder: name	
		• Amazon KDE management (Nia): worked on test prints	
		• Sales oversight (Carlos):	
		○ numbers look good!	
		○ Did some geographical analysis	
		• Customer service (Oliver):	
		○ Regular complaints...	
		• Design (Aaliyah): worked template for new series	
		• Packaging and supplies (Nia) - (absent)	
00:30	5	**User Review and Rating System**	Report ˅
		• Database structure	
		• User interface design	
		• Star rating system	
		• Text review input	
		• Review moderation	
		Question: What about User verification? → worked on next	

(handwritten annotations:) check off tasks · let roles and links type their own notes or type what they report (keywords) · helps stay on time · choose desired outcome · write brief keyword of what has been reported

(This assumes a meeting that mixes operational and policy decisions in one meeting. Adjust accordingly if your organization separates operation and policies in separate meetings.)

Sociocracy For All

00:35	10	**Recommendation Engine**	Decision ⏷

Proposal:

Institute a recommendation engine for our digital booklet platform. The objective is to personalize the user experience by suggesting relevant booklet titles based on their browsing history, past purchases, and booklet ratings.

Objectives:

- *Improve user engagement and retention*
- *Increase conversion rates and sales*

Full link for projected numbers

Term: Dec 2023

Questions
Numbers for objectives? Answer: see spreadsheet

records reactions, final wording and decision ✍️

Reactions

- Sounds great!
- A little worried about amount of work. Is it worth it?

→ consent!

0:45	10	**Booklet Preview Feature (Carlos)**	Exploration ⏷

Carlos wants to talk to website circle about integration to improve sales. Reactions?

- Will there be a preview page limit? What about copyright protection?
- Text and image quality appropriate?
- Cool idea, should be useful! Love page flipping animations, very engaging.
- Ask them about experience re user experience (UX)
- Useful to see an integration with product page

notes for Carlos for reference ✍️

0:55	1	**ACTION ITEMS RECAP** – to paste under next meeting's *Action Items Accountability*	Report

- ☐ Carlos to talk to website circle

new action items , add to list on top for next time ✍️

0:56	1	**BACKLOG UPDATE** – added directly	Exploration

0:57	4	**CLOSING ROUND / CHECK-OUT** – feedback on content, interpersonal, processes	

- Sad Nia wasn't here, hope she's ok
- Excited about new projects
- Great use of rounds

Meetings from previous meetings are in the same document:

2023-05-29

TIME & DURATION   MEETING'S LOCATION/LINK   OUTCOME

Supporting proposals

Be proactive!

Instead of just typing notes, try to synthesize ideas into proposals that capture the spirit of the meeting into a shared document. That way, the facilitator can work off your proposal - a huge contribution to the effectiveness and clarity of a meeting!

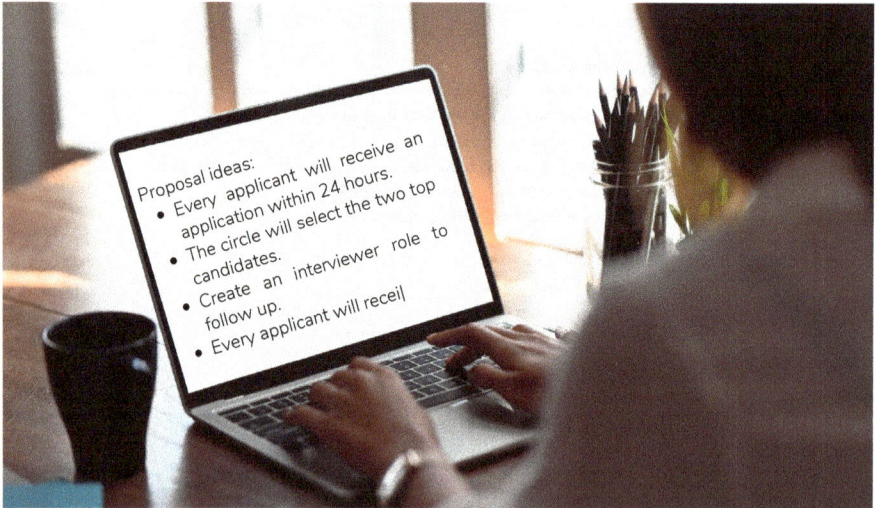

The backlog

The backlog is one central place where we list future agenda items. They are different from tasks.

Tasks

actions steps we've already agreed to; there's no talking needed; they simply need to be done. Many circles track them on a separate list or in a task management tool.

Backlog items

future discussion topics, reports, decisions, or reviews that we need to take time to do in a meeting. They are typically tracked by the circle secretary in collaboration with the leader.

During the circle meetings, identify the tasks and the future agenda items that emerge from the meeting and write them in the appropriate places.

Backlog

Review dates:
- June 2024 Membership Policy
- April 2025 ACE policy

Role term ends:
- June 2026: facilitator, delegate
- November 2026: leader, secretary
- April 2025: ACE manager

Future agenda items:
- additional membership category?
- how to increase accountability on ACE
- conversion rate improve how?
- give feedback to Data Circle

Some circles organize the backlog into different categories

Supporting secretaries

- Ideally, others read along while the secretary is writing. If the secretary is behind, wait or support.
- Some groups have an appointed backup secretary that can type while the secretary is speaking as a circle member. They might also follow the secretary and clean up the notes.
- Make agreements on whether others can type in the document. Sometimes other members want to type up a proposal that they have in mind, which can lead to tensions because it might confuse the secretary.
- While processing proposals, it is a good idea to give secretaries time to complete writing a proposal up, then read it (maybe even out loud) - if the circle rushes ahead, they might not be clear what they actually decided.

Who prepares the meetings?

The secretary prepares the agenda document.

For planning the actual agenda, every circle makes their own policy on meeting preparation. The standard way is for the facilitator, leader, and secretary to prepare a meeting agenda. The idea is that the leader has an idea of the future of the circle's work, while the secretary holds the circle's records from the past and the facilitator is situated in the present of the circle's process. Each contributes to planning a meeting that connects all parts, moving the circle forward.

What if note-taking slows down the meeting?

A circle will sometimes have to wait for the secretary to note down a proposal or an idea (for example, proposal ideas during proposal shaping which is a lot to write down fast). Make sure they are supported well enough so they can also participate as circle members.

If the circle does not want to slow down, find a way to modify your process. You can appoint two people to take notes (taking turns), or – if you work in a shared document – you can have people type their own ideas.

Overall, keep in mind that while it's the secretary's role, the circle shares the responsibility to find and maintain a workable solution to note taking.

Find templates!

You can find the templates on our website.
www.sociocracyforall.org/templates

Sociocracy For All

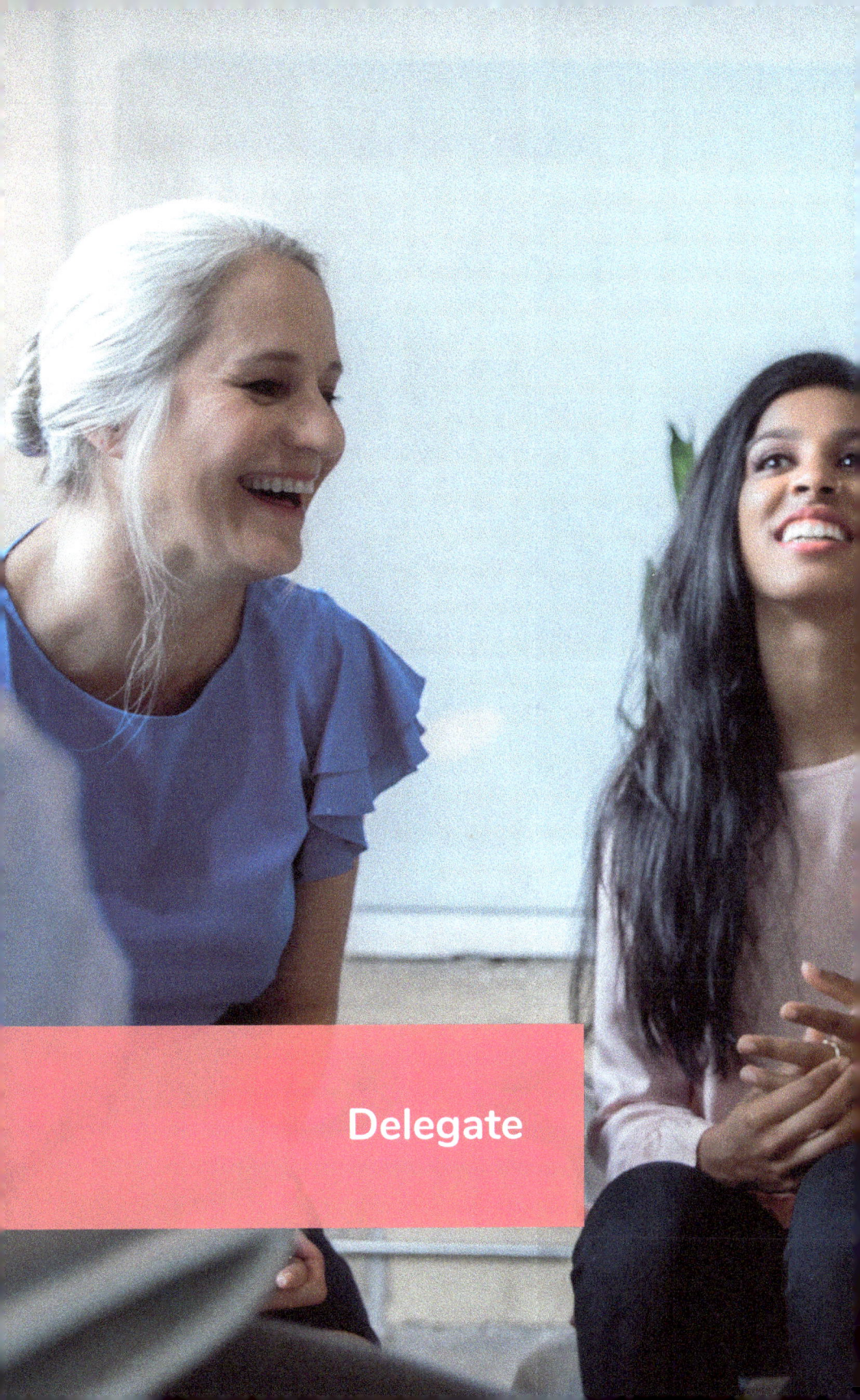

Delegate

What do delegates do?

Delegates carry the voice of the circle into the next-higher circle. That means you report in the parent circle.

Be sure to be prepared to do the reporting, ideally by re-reading your circle's notes or other relevant information.

In the parent circle meetings, ask yourself:
How do the things that we talk about in the circle affect the wider organization?

In your circle meetings, ask yourself:
What does the parent circle need to know about what's going on in my circle?

Reporting directions

It can be confusing at first to figure out who reports where. Let's look at an example!

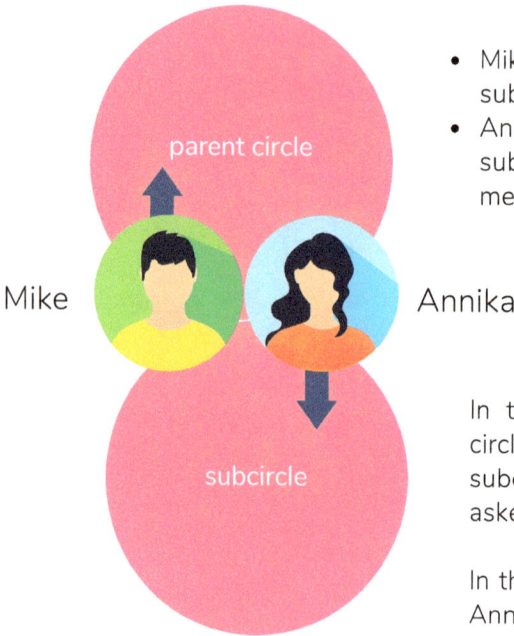

- Mike is delegate from the subcircle to the parent circle.
- Annika is the leader of the subcircle (and therefore also a member in the parent circle).

In the meetings of the parent circle, Mike reports about the subcircle and Annika might be asked to add.

In the meetings of the subcircle, Annika reports about the parent circle (and Mike might be asked to add).

Filter and amplify

Both leaders and delegates report between circles. In doing so, they filter out information that is too detailed to pass on. They amplify pieces of information that might look insignificant but are part of a bigger pattern.

For example, if people in the circle are not getting tasks done more often than before, this might just be a coincidence. Or it might be part of an unhealthy pattern that is forming. In that case, raising it before it becomes a real problem might be helpful, in particular, if other circles report the same emerging pattern.

filter

details
information
details
information
details

information

information

amplify

detail

information!

Useful questions for delegates

Take your reporting function seriously. Information is of high value in a sociocratic organization - it's our way of knowing what's going on, and our way to catch little issues before they become big problems.

- Review the notes of the circle you're reporting from. What topics need to be reported "up"?
- How is the circle really doing? How's the mood, the productivity, workload, and connection among the people?
- Is there anything you're noticing that seems off? Does the leader seem to represent the other circle accurately? What else needs to be said?
- Is there an accomplishment that you want to celebrate? Spread the joy!

? What are your thoughts on rotating delegates?

It is hard to get into the swing of things with rotating roles. For delegates, this is an even bigger issue because they are part of two circles. The people filling the role as a delegate in the parent circle will only have spotty knowledge of the parent circle's arch of conversation which makes it a tricky situation to be effective in.

? How long should a report take?

Some organizations simply type reports and say highlights out loud. Others do reporting verbally. A report should not be longer than 2-3 minutes.

Organization-wide roles

Organization-wide roles

Just like there are roles that need to be held in every circle to help the circle function, there are also roles that can help the organization as a whole function.

The most important role is the **logbook keeper**. That is the role of the person that makes sure that ALL circle policies are current and accessible. It's basically the secretary of the whole organization.

That person might also be in charge of maintaining the system that stores roles and circles with their aims in a visual diagram so everyone can look up everyone's roles in the organization.

There are similar functions like that, like the strategy role or roles related to the organization-wide finances.

Sometimes, that function is held by a circle, for example, a process, finance or membership circle, or it is a role in the General Circle.

Since sociocracy is such a flexible system that can easily be tailored to your needs, pay attention to what is falling through the cracks and then make a plan to address it by creating roles in the appropriate circle(s).

Don't shy away from creative and innovative solutions - as long as you evaluate how they are working out!

Other circle roles

What other roles might be useful?

Do you think you need more roles?

Here's a distinction that will clarify what kinds of roles you need:

- **Circle roles** are process related. Every circle needs them, independent of the work. Examples are the roles in this booklet.
    - A leader is needed to make sure all operations of the circle (whatever they are) get done.
    - A facilitator makes sure meetings can be held.
    - A secretary makes sure notes are taken and documents are in order.
    - A delegate makes sure the circle is connected to the rest of the organization.

- **Operational roles** are unique to the circle and related to tasks and responsibilities of the specific circle's work. For example, books sales manager, website admin, customer support.
    - Define them by defining the tasks, activities or accountabilities, decisions they can make and listing policies and workflows they are guided by. You can also add connections they have with other roles in the organization (operational handoffs).
    - Learn more in our other booklets with examples.

For most circles, the given circle (process) roles are enough. But if you want to add more, you can do that of course! In that case, all circles in your organization might add that role.

Here are some examples of circle roles in addition.

- Timekeeper. That can be useful if facilitators are overwhelmed by tracking time in addition to facilitating.
- Tuner. Some organizations have designated tuners that make proposals out of proposal ideas that they hear.
- Emotional support. That can be useful in case there's a lot of emotional support needed and the leader is overwhelmed with extra support needed by circle members.
- Financial admin. If circles have to take care of their own budgets, you might want to define that role and make sure all circles have someone who fills that role.
- Conflict resolution point person or ombuds-person.
- Metrics manager. Tracks and reports on objectives and key results in the circle.
- Wisdom keepers. If you want to make sure all decisions in all circles are aligned with your value set, you can assign perspectives for all circles. Examples:
  - 7 Generations
  - DEI
  - Nature's voice

Watch out, every additional role creates overhead with term ends, selections and reviews, so only add roles that you are sure will add value.

You can also modify existing roles and widen them. For example, you can add conflict resolution or emotional support as a responsibility of the delegate, or time keeping in the leader. That's a good idea to keep things simple.

In that case, write a role description for the role in your organization that modified the default of the role descriptions on the following pages.

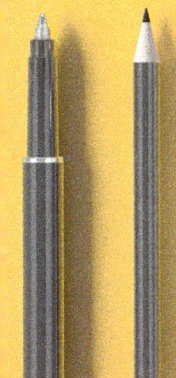

Role description templates

Leader

- Oversees operations in the circle and progress toward the aim
- Supports roles in performing their tasks
- Member of the parent circle
- Reports from parent circle
- Prepares the meeting agenda (with the facilitator and/or secretary)

Additions/modifications:

Delegate

- Member of the parent circle
- Reports to parent circle

Additions/modifications:

Facilitator

- Moderates circle meetings
- Focuses on equal voice and efficiency
- Supports preparation of the meeting agenda (with the leader and/or secretary)

Additions/modifications:

Secretary

- Keeps circle notes
- Maintains circle documents like circle minutes, documentation, backlog etc.
- Supports meetings by developing proposals in collaboration with the facilitator and other circle members.

Additions/modifications:

Performance reviews
for roles

Asking for feedback

We highly recommend instituting a way to get feedback on your circle roles.

After all, the circle roles exist to support the functioning of the circle - so it makes sense to find out whether the circle feels supported enough, and whether there are ways to do it even better.

A super simple format is to ask for feedback in a round. That takes about 5-15 minutes and gives you more information.

You can also look up full performance reviews (but they will likely be too much for a simple circle roles).

A simple way to remember and make it a healthy habit is to schedule the feedback session at the same time when you get selected.

Example: you get selected as facilitator in June for a 12-month term. The new selection date should go on the backlog for June next year. But also schedule a feedback session in October - that way you can get used to the role and then learn from the feedback and improve even more for the rest of the term.

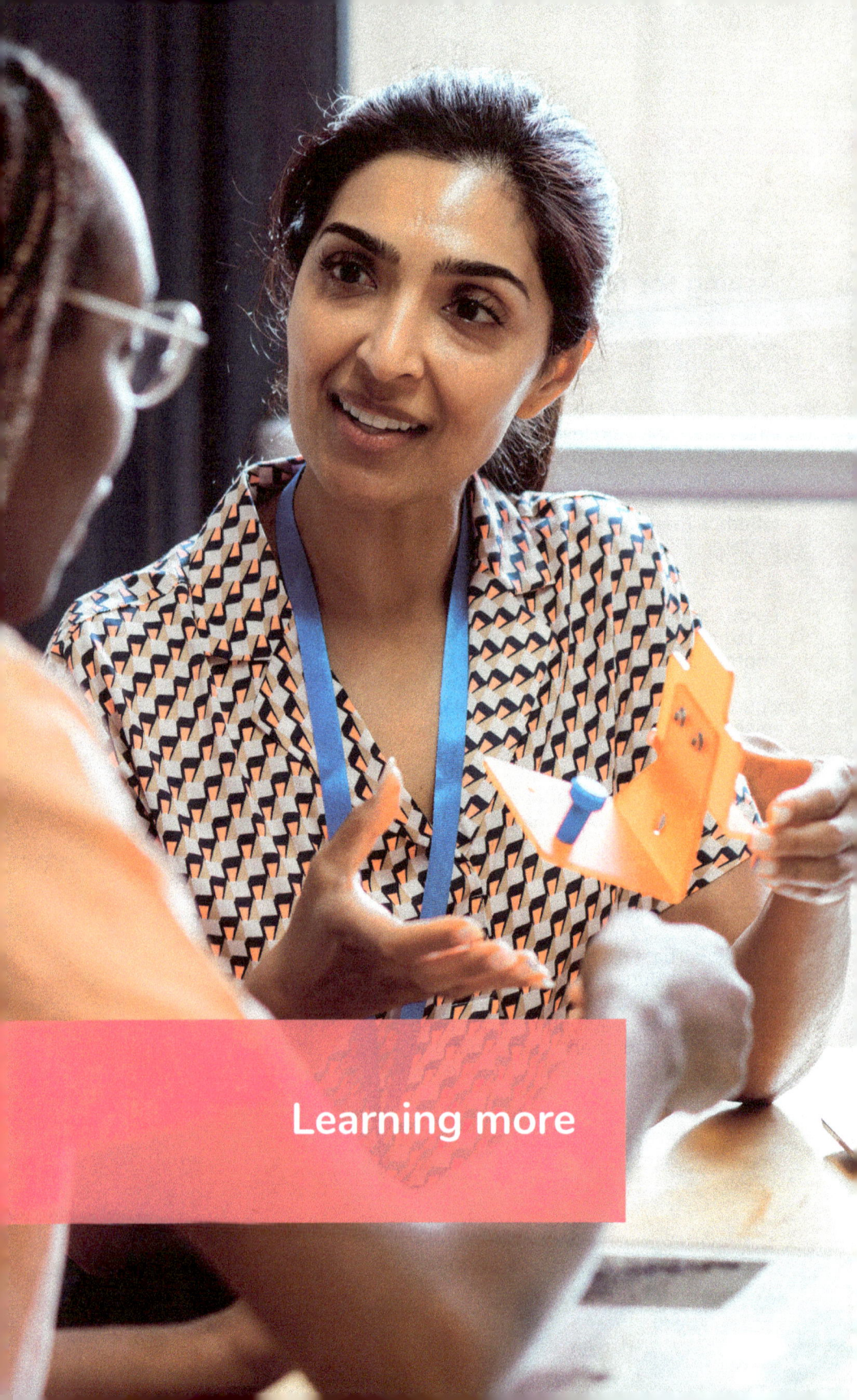

Learning more

Offerings

Facilitation
We can facilitate your Board retreat, performance reviews, strategic planning process, conflict engagement, any team that is having a difficult time, or just model and run a sociocratic meeting.

Organizational Structure Redesign
We can help you redesign your organizational structure to better implement sociocracy or to adapt to changing circumstances.

Organizational Audit
We can assess the quality of your current functioning, suggest an improvement plan, and help you carry it out, even if you are not already a sociocratic organization.

Implementing Sociocracy
We can support you from the beginning to the end of the process of adopting sociocracy.

www.sociocracyforall.org/coaching

Books (full books)

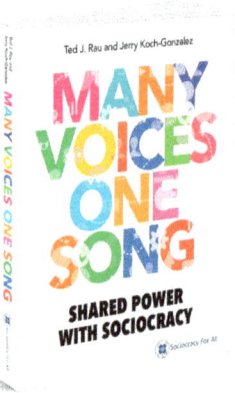

The manual about sociocracy. Packed with information, examples, diagrams and an index. Find deeper explanations about all the processes and situations.

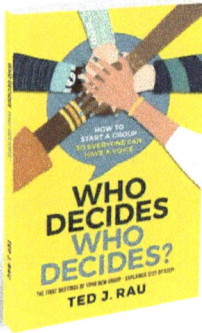

A simple step-by-step guide for starting a group sociocratically. Best for groups 2-12 people.

Educators and parents!
Use sociocracy with children to teach responsible and caring decision-making.

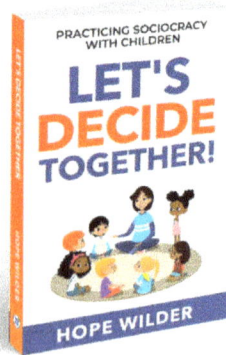

www.sociocracyforall.org/books

Small booklets in this series

For facilitators
(70 pages)

A summary for
role holders (70 pages)

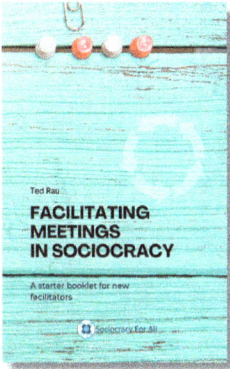

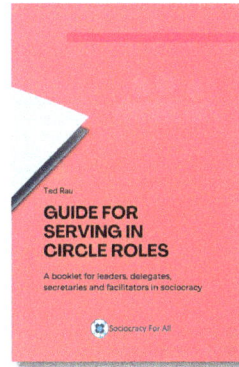

>> www.sociocracyforall.org/books

Cards

Bored with your closing
rounds? Try out our card
decks of check-out prompts!

They include feedback on
- **process**
- **content**
- **interpersonal**

www.sociocracyforall.org/cards

Sociocracy For All

Sociocracy For All is a member-run nonprofit that offers training and consulting for individuals and groups at all levels.

Topics:
- Decision-making by consent
- Organizational structure
- Inclusive meetings
- Performance and accountability

- Facilitation practice
- Immersion programs
- Conflict resolution
- Nonviolent Communication for meeting facilitation
- Certification programs

See our training offerings: www.sociocracyforall.org/training